I0448781

July 2013

INVESTMENT ADVISERS

Requirements and Costs Associated with the Custody Rule

July 2013

INVESTMENT ADVISERS

Requirements and Costs Associated with the Custody Rule

Why GAO Did This Study

Investment advisers provide a wide range of services and collectively manage around $54 trillion in assets for around 24 million clients. Unlike banks and broker-dealers, investment advisers typically do not maintain physical custody of client assets. However, under federal securities regulations, advisers may be deemed to have custody because of their authority to access client assets, for example, by deducting advisory fees from a client account. High-profile fraud cases in recent years highlighted the risks faced by investors when an adviser has custody of their assets. In response, SEC amended its custody rule in 2009 to require a broader range of advisers to undergo annual surprise examinations by independent accountants. At the same time, SEC provided relief from this requirement to certain advisers, including those deemed to have custody solely because of their use of related but "operationally independent" custodians. The Dodd-Frank Wall Street Reform and Consumer Protection Act mandates GAO to study the costs associated with the custody rule. This report describes (1) the requirements of and costs associated with the custody rule and (2) SEC's rationale for not requiring advisers using related but operationally independent custodians to undergo surprise examinations.

To address the objectives, GAO reviewed federal securities laws and related rules, analyzed data on advisers, and met with SEC, advisers, accounting firms, and industry and other associations.

View GAO-13-569. For more information, contact A. Nicole Clowers at (202) 512-8678 or clowersa@gao.gov.

What GAO Found

Designed to safeguard client assets, the Securities and Exchange Commission's (SEC) rule governing advisers' custody of client assets (custody rule) imposes various requirements and, in turn, costs on investment advisers. To protect investors, the rule requires advisers that have custody to (1) use qualified custodians (e.g., banks or broker-dealers) to hold client assets and (2) have a reasonable basis for believing that the custodian sends account statements directly to clients.

The rule also requires advisers with custody, unless they qualify for an exception, to hire an independent public accountant to conduct annually a surprise examination to verify custody of client assets. According to accountants that GAO interviewed, examination cost depends on an adviser's number of clients under custody and other factors. These factors vary widely across advisers that currently report undergoing surprise examinations: for example, their reported number of clients under custody ranged from 1 client to over 1 million clients as of April 2013. Thus, the cost of the examinations varies widely across the advisers. The rule also requires advisers maintaining client assets or using a qualified custodian that is a related person to obtain an internal control report to assess the suitability and effectiveness of controls in place. The cost of these reports varies across custodians based on their size and services.

SEC provided an exception from the surprise examination requirement to, among others, advisers deemed to have custody solely because of their use of related but "operationally independent" custodians. According to SEC, an adviser and custodian under common ownership but having operationally independent management pose relatively lower client custodial risks, because the misuse of client assets would tend to require collusion between the firms' employees. To be considered operationally independent, an adviser and its related custodian must not be under common supervision, not share premises, and meet other conditions. About 2 percent of the SEC-registered advisers qualify for this exception for at least some of their clients. If the exception were eliminated, the cost of the surprise examination would vary across the advisers because the factors that affect examination cost vary widely across the advisers.

Number of SEC-Registered Investment Advisers, as of April 2013

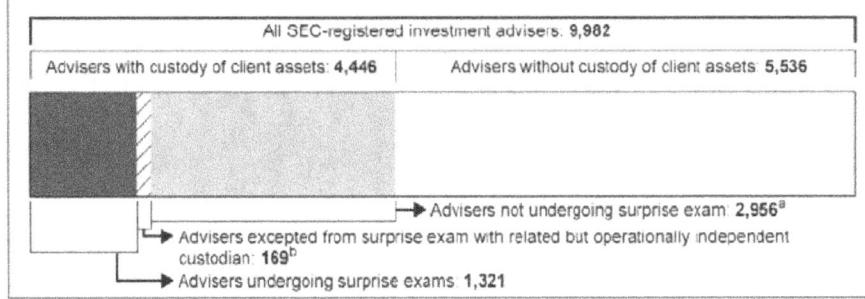

Source: GAO analysis of Form ADV data as of April 1, 2013.

[a]These advisers may undergo an annual financial statement audit in lieu of a surprise examination.

[b]Of the 169 SEC-registered investment advisers excepted from the surprise examination requirement, 41 of them qualified for an exception from the surprise examination requirement for some of their clients under custody but underwent a surprise examination for other clients under custody.

_____ **United States Government Accountability Office**

Contents

Abbreviations

IARD	Investment Adviser Registration Depository
NASAA	North American Securities Administrators Association
PCAOB	Public Company Accounting Oversight Board
SEC	Securities and Exchange Commission

GAO

U.S. GOVERNMENT ACCOUNTABILITY OFFICE

441 G St. N.W.
Washington, DC 20548

July 8, 2013

The Honorable Tim Johnson
Chairman
The Honorable Mike Crapo
Ranking Member
Committee on Banking, Housing, and Urban Affairs
United States Senate

The Honorable Jeb Hensarling
Chairman
The Honorable Maxine Waters
Ranking Member
Committee on Financial Services
House of Representatives

Investment advisers provide a wide range of investment advisory services and collectively manage around $54 trillion in assets for about 24 million clients. Unlike banks and broker-dealers, investment advisers typically do not maintain physical custody of client assets—that is, client funds and securities. However, under federal securities regulations, advisers may be deemed to have custody because of their authority to access client assets, for example, by deducting advisory fees from a client account.[1] The collapse of Bernard L. Madoff Investment Securities, LLC—an investment adviser and broker-dealer—in December 2008 resulted in thousands of investors losing over $50 billion and highlighted the risks investors face when an adviser has custody of client funds and securities.

Under the Securities and Exchange Commission's (SEC) custody rule, advisers that have custody of client assets are required to implement controls designed to protect those assets from being lost, misused, misappropriated, or subject to the advisers' financial reverses, such as insolvency.[2] SEC first adopted the custody rule in 1962, after Congress amended the Investment Advisers Act of 1940 (Advisers Act) in 1960 to give it authority to promulgate rules to define and prescribe means reasonably designed to prevent fraudulent, deceptive, or manipulative

---

[1] 17 C.F.R. § 275.206(4)-2(d)(2).

[2] See 75 Fed. Reg. 1456, 1457, 1475 (2010).

GAO-13-569 SEC Custody Rule Costs

acts, practices, or courses of business.[3] At that time, the rule generally required, among other things, that advisers with custody hire an independent public accountant to conduct an annual surprise examination to verify custody of client assets. In 2003, SEC amended the rule to require advisers to adopt new controls to protect client assets and relieve certain advisers from the surprise examination requirement.[4] In response to the Madoff and other recent frauds, SEC amended the rule again in 2009 to improve the safekeeping of client assets—in part by expanding the surprise examination requirement's reach.[5] As noted by SEC in its 2009 final rule adopting release, surprise examinations provide "another set of eyes" on client assets and thus additional protection against their misappropriation. Under the amended rule, SEC continued to provide an exception from the surprise examination requirement to certain advisers, including advisers that have custody solely because of their use of related but "operationally independent" custodians to hold client assets.[6]

Section 412 of the Dodd-Frank Wall Street Reform and Consumer Protection Act mandates us to study the costs that investment advisers registered with SEC incur to comply with SEC's record-keeping and custody rules, as well as the additional costs that advisers would incur if the operationally independent exception were eliminated.[7] This report describes

---

[3]15 U.S.C. § 80b-6(4) (added by Pub. L. No. 86-750, sec. 9, 74 Stat. 885, 887 (1960)); Adoption of Rule 206(4)-2, Investment Advisers Act Release No. 123, 1962 SEC LEXIS 655 (Feb. 27, 1962).

[4]Custody of Funds or Securities of Clients by Investment Advisers, Investment Advisers Act Release No. 2176, 68 Fed. Reg. 56,692 (Oct. 1, 2003). Under the amended rule, advisers with custody of client assets were required to maintain the assets with qualified custodians. If the qualified custodian sent account statements directly to the adviser's clients at least quarterly, the adviser was relieved from having to send its own account statements and undergo an annual surprise examination.

[5]Custody of Funds or Securities of Clients by Investment Advisers, Investment Advisers Act Release No. 2968 (Dec. 30, 2009), 75 Fed. Reg. 1456 (Jan. 11, 2010).

[6]In the rule, SEC has set out a number of conditions that an adviser must meet to satisfy the definition of "operationally independent." We discuss those conditions in detail later in this report.

[7]Pub. L. No. 111-203, § 412, 124 Stat.1376, 1577 (2010).

GAO-13-569 SEC Custody Rule Costs

- the requirements of and costs associated with the SEC custody rule, including any related record-keeping requirements, for registered investment advisers; and
- SEC's rationale for not requiring advisers using related but operationally independent custodians to undergo surprise examinations, and the number and characteristics of such advisers.

To address these objectives, we reviewed and analyzed the Advisers Act and related regulations; proposed and final amendments made to SEC's custody rule, including comment letters; and relevant GAO, SEC, industry, and academic studies on investment advisers. We also analyzed publicly available Form ADV data filed by investment advisers to determine, among other things, the number of SEC-registered investment advisers that reported complying with certain custody rule requirements, including the surprise examination requirement, and assess the characteristics of certain investment advisers.[8] We interviewed SEC staff about the controls and procedures used to ensure the reliability of the data and found the data to be sufficiently reliable for the purposes of our report.

To obtain data on costs of complying with the SEC custody rule, particularly its surprise examination and internal control report requirements, we selected 12 investment advisers based on the number of their client accounts and amount of assets under custody. We interviewed eight of the advisers and four accounting firms that had conducted surprise examinations for the 12 selected advisers to obtain data on surprise examination costs and, if applicable, internal control reports. To obtain information about the requirements, costs, and other issues associated with the SEC custody rule, we interviewed, among others, federal and state regulators and representatives from various industry and other associations. (See app. I for more information about our scope and methodology.)

We conducted this performance audit from September 2012 through July 2013 in accordance with generally accepted government auditing

---

[8]Form ADV is the form used by investment advisers to register with both SEC and state securities authorities. Form ADV consists of two parts. Part 1 collects information about the adviser's business, ownership, clients, employees, business practices (especially those involving potential conflicts with clients), and any disciplinary events of the adviser or its employees. Part 2 collects information from client brochures and brochure supplements.

standards. Those standards require that we plan and perform the audit to obtain sufficient, appropriate evidence to provide a reasonable basis for our findings and conclusions based on our audit objectives. We believe that the evidence obtained provides a reasonable basis for our findings and conclusions based on our audit objectives.

Background

Investment advisers provide a wide range of investment advisory services and help individuals and institutions make financial decisions.[9] From individuals and families seeking to plan for retirement or save for college to large institutions managing billions of dollars, clients seek the services of investment advisers to help them evaluate their investment needs, plan for their future, and develop and implement investment strategies. Advisers can include money managers, investment consultants, and financial planners. They commonly manage the investment portfolios of individuals, businesses, and pooled investment vehicles, such as mutual funds, pension funds, and hedge and other private funds. Many investment advisers also engage in other businesses, such as insurance broker or broker-dealer services. Many investment advisers charge clients fees for investment advisory services based on the percentage of assets under management, but others may charge hourly or fixed rates and, in certain circumstances, performance fees.

The Advisers Act generally defines an investment adviser, with certain exceptions, as any individual or firm that for compensation engages in the business of advising others, either directly or through publications or writings, as to the value of securities or as to the advisability of investing in, purchasing, or selling securities.[10] An entity that falls within the definition of "investment adviser" must register under the Advisers Act, unless it (1) is a small firm regulated by one or more of the states and thus prohibited from registering or (2) qualifies for an exemption from the

---

[9]For additional information about investment advisers, see SEC, *Study on Investment Advisers and Broker-Dealers, as Required by Section 913 of the Dodd-Frank Wall Street Reform and Consumer Protection Act* (Washington, D.C.: January 2011).

[10]15 U.S.C. § 80b-2(a)(11).

Advisers Act's registration requirement.[11] The Advisers Act imposes a broad fiduciary duty on advisers to act in the best interest of their clients.

Most small- and mid-sized advisers are regulated by the states and prohibited from registering with SEC.[12] Large advisers who do not meet an exemption from registration must register with SEC. To register, applicants file a Form ADV with SEC. Once registered, an adviser must update the form at least annually. SEC-registered advisers are subject to five types of requirements: (1) fiduciary duties to clients; (2) substantive prohibitions and requirements, including that advisers with custody of client assets take steps designed to safeguard those client assets; (3) contractual requirements; (4) record-keeping requirements; and (5) oversight by SEC.

SEC oversees registered investment advisers primarily through its Office of Compliance Inspections and Examinations, Division of Investment Management, and Division of Enforcement. Specifically, the Office of Compliance Inspections and Examinations examines investment advisers to evaluate their compliance with federal securities laws, determines whether these firms are fulfilling their fiduciary duty to clients and operating in accordance with disclosures made to investors and contractual obligations, and assesses the effectiveness of their compliance-control systems. The Division of Investment Management administers the securities laws affecting investment advisers and engages in rule making for consideration by SEC and other policy initiatives that are intended, among other things, to strengthen SEC's oversight of investment advisers. The Division of Enforcement

---

[11]See 15 U.S.C. §§ 80b-3, 80b-3a. For a more detailed discussion, see SEC, Investment Adviser Regulation Office, Division of Investment Management, Regulation of Investment Advisers (March 2013).

[12]15 U.S.C. § 80b-3a. Unless an exemption is available, all advisers with their principal office and place of business in Wyoming and mid-sized advisers with their principal office and place of business in New York are not "subject to examination" and must register with SEC. In terms of regulatory assets under management, small-sized advisers generally have less than $25 million, mid-sized generally more than $25 million but less than $100 million, and large-sized generally more than $100 million. Regulatory assets under management are the sum of assets under management or securities portfolios for which the adviser provides continuous and regular supervisory or management services and include, for accounts of private funds, the amount of any uncalled capital commitments as of the date of filing. Advisers are instructed to determine the amount based on the current market value of the assets as determined within 90 days prior to the date of filing.

GAO-13-569 SEC Custody Rule Costs

investigates and prosecutes certain violations of securities laws and regulations.

Nearly 10,000 advisers were registered with SEC as of April 1, 2013.[13] Collectively, these advisers managed nearly $54 trillion in assets for about 24 million clients. The majority of these SEC-registered advisers each managed less than $1 billion in assets, and a majority had 100 or fewer clients. Specifically, as shown in figure 1, about 71 percent of the registered advisers (around 7,133 advisers) managed less than $1 billion in assets. Furthermore, the largest 94 registered advisers (about 1 percent of all SEC-registered advisers) managed about 50 percent of the total regulatory assets under management.

Figure 1: Percentage of SEC-Registered Advisers by Amount of Regulatory Assets under Management, as of April 1, 2013

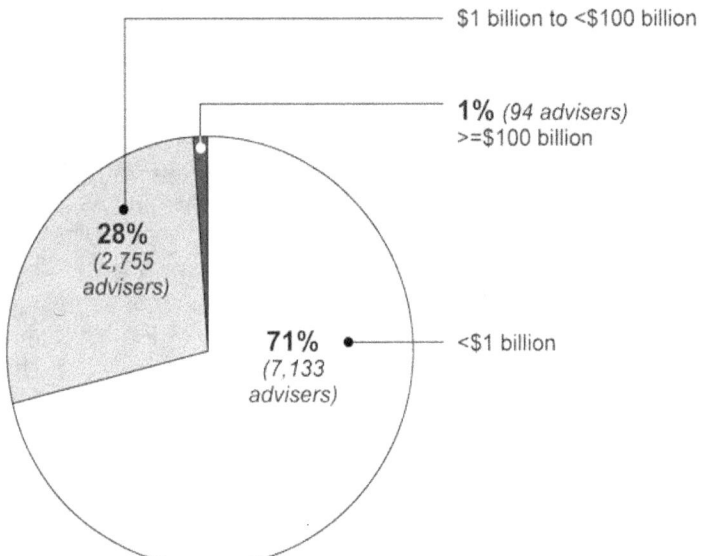

Source: GAO analysis of Form ADV data as of April 1, 2013.

Notes: Regulatory assets under management are the sum of assets under management or securities portfolios for which the adviser provides continuous and regular supervisory or management services

[13]The statistics are based on Form ADV data. We excluded from our statistics advisers that had not filed updated Form ADV information since December 1, 2011, and advisers that reported no, or zero, regulatory assets under management or advisory clients.

GAO-13-569 SEC Custody Rule Costs

and include, for accounts of private funds, the amount of any uncalled capital commitments as of the date of filing. Advisers are instructed to determine the amount based on the current market value of the assets as determined within 90 days prior to the date of filing.

In addition, as shown in figure 2, about 6,000 registered advisers (nearly 60 percent of all registered advisers) reported having 100 or fewer clients, while approximately 1,200 advisers (around 12 percent of all registered advisers) reported having more than 500 clients.

Figure 2: Distribution of SEC-Registered Advisers by Number of Clients, as of April 1, 2013

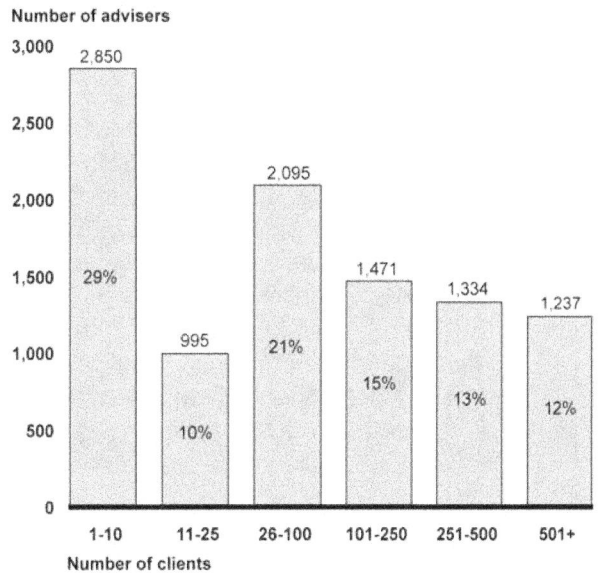

Source: GAO analysis of Form ADV data as of April 1, 2013.

Custody Rule Requirements and Compliance Costs Vary across Advisers

SEC-registered investment advisers with custody of client assets are required by the SEC custody rule to comply with a number of requirements designed to safeguard client assets. Under the rule, an adviser has custody if it holds, directly or indirectly, client funds or securities or has any authority to obtain possession of them.[14] An adviser also has custody if a related person of the adviser holds, directly or

---

[14]17 C.F.R. § 275.206(4)-2(d)(2).

indirectly, client funds or securities or has any authority to obtain possession of them, in connection with advisory services provided by the adviser to the client.[15] Custody includes:

- possession of client funds or securities;
- any capacity that gives the adviser legal ownership or access to client assets, for example, as a general partner of a limited partnership, managing member of a limited liability company, or a comparable position for another pooled investment vehicle (e.g., hedge fund); or
- any arrangement, including a general power of attorney, under which the adviser is authorized or permitted to withdraw client funds or securities maintained with a custodian upon its instruction to the custodian.

Custody Rule Requirements Are Intended to Safeguard Client Assets

SEC's custody rule regulates the custody practices of investment advisers and contains a number of investor protections. The rule requires advisers that have custody to maintain client assets with a "qualified custodian," which includes banks and savings associations, registered broker-dealers, registered futures commission merchants, and certain foreign financial institutions.[16] This requirement, along with other parts of the rule, helps prevent client assets from being lost or stolen. Furthermore, qualified custodians are subject to regulation and oversight by federal financial regulators and self-regulatory organizations.[17] Some registered advisers also engage in other businesses, such as broker-dealers that provide custodial services to themselves or related advisers.

[15]*Id.* A related person includes anyone who controls, is controlled by, or is under common control with the adviser. 17 C.F.R. § 275.206(4)-2(d)(7).

[16]17 C.F.R. § 275.206(4)-2(d)(6). Entities that can serve as custodians include: brokers, which are in the business of effecting transactions in securities for the account of others; dealers, which are in the business of buying and selling securities for their own account through a broker or otherwise; and futures commission merchants which solicit or accept orders for the purchase or sale of any commodity for future delivery on or subject to the rules of any exchange and that accept payment from or extend credit to those whose orders are accepted.

[17]For example, banks are regulated by the prudential regulators; registered broker-dealers are regulated by SEC and the Financial Industry Regulatory Authority; and registered futures commission merchants are regulated by the Commodity Futures Trading Commission and National Futures Association.

The rule requires advisers that have custody of client assets to have a reasonable basis, after due inquiry, for believing that the custodian sends periodic statements directly to the clients.[18] An adviser can satisfy the due-inquiry requirement in a number of ways, such as by receiving a copy of the account statements sent to the clients or written confirmation from the custodian that account statements were sent to the adviser's clients. This requirement serves to help assure the integrity of account statements and permit clients to identify any erroneous or unauthorized transactions or withdrawals by an adviser. If an adviser also elects to send its own clients account statements, it must include a note urging its clients to compare the custodian's and adviser's account statements.

Surprise Examinations

The SEC custody rule requires advisers with custody of client assets to hire an independent public accountant to conduct an annual surprise examination, unless the advisers qualify for an exception.[19] A surprise examination is intended to help deter and detect fraudulent activity by having an independent accountant verify that client assets—of which an adviser has custody—are held by a qualified custodian in an appropriate account and in the correct amount. The accountant determines the time of the examination without prior notice to the adviser, and the accountant is to vary the timing of the examination from year to year. SEC initially required all advisers to undergo surprise examinations when it adopted the custody rule in 1962.[20] Over the following decades of administering the custody rule, SEC staff provided no-action relief from the surprise examination requirement where other substitute client safeguards were implemented. In 2003, SEC amended the custody rule by generally requiring an adviser to maintain client assets with qualified custodians and relieving the adviser from the examination requirement if its qualified custodian sent account statements directly to the adviser's clients.[21] In its proposed rule at that time, SEC noted that the examination was performed only annually, and many months could pass before the accountant had an opportunity to detect a fraud.[22] In its 2009 proposed

---

[18]17 C.F.R. § 275.206(4)-2(a)(3).

[19]17 C.F.R. § 275.206(4)-2(a)(4).

[20]Adoption of Rule 206(4)-2, Investment Advisers Act Release No. 123, 1962 SEC LEXIS 655 (Feb. 27, 1962).

[21]68 Fed. Reg. 56,692 (Oct. 1, 2003).

[22]67 Fed. Reg. 48,579, 48,583 (July 25, 2002).

amendments, SEC revisited the 2003 rule making in light of its significant enforcement actions alleging misappropriation of client assets.[23] In expanding the surprise examination requirement, SEC noted that an independent public accountant may identify misuse that clients have not, which would result in the earlier detection of fraudulent activities and reduce resulting client losses.[24]

While SEC expanded the reach of the surprise examination requirement in its final 2009 rule amendments, it provided several exceptions to the requirement. As shown in figure 3, advisers meeting the following conditions may not be required to undergo a surprise examination:

- an adviser that is deemed to have custody of client assets solely because of its authority to deduct fees from client accounts;
- an adviser that is deemed to have custody because a related person has custody, and the adviser is "operationally independent" of the related person serving as the custodian;[25] or
- an adviser to a pooled investment vehicle (e.g., hedge fund) that is subject to an annual financial statement audit by an independent public accountant registered with and subject to regular inspection by the Public Company Accounting Oversight Board (PCAOB) and distributes the audited financial statements prepared in accordance with generally accepted accounting principles to its clients is deemed to have satisfied the surprise examination requirement.[26]

---

[23]74 Fed. Reg. 25,354, 25,355 (May 27, 2009).

[24]Id. at 25,356.

[25]According to SEC, an adviser that has custody for reasons that are separate from having an operationally independent related person with custody may be subject to the surprise examination requirement.

[26]PCAOB is a nonprofit corporation established by Congress to oversee the audits of public companies in order to protect the interests of investors and further the public interest in the preparation of informative, accurate, and independent audit reports. PCAOB also oversees the audits of broker-dealers, including compliance reports filed pursuant to federal securities laws, to promote investor protection. In addition, the SEC custody rule requires advisers to pooled investment vehicles that comply with the rule by distributing audited financial statements to investors to also obtain an audit upon liquidation of the pool when the liquidation occurs before the fund's fiscal year-end.

Figure 3: Exceptions to the Surprise Examination or Internal Control Report Requirements

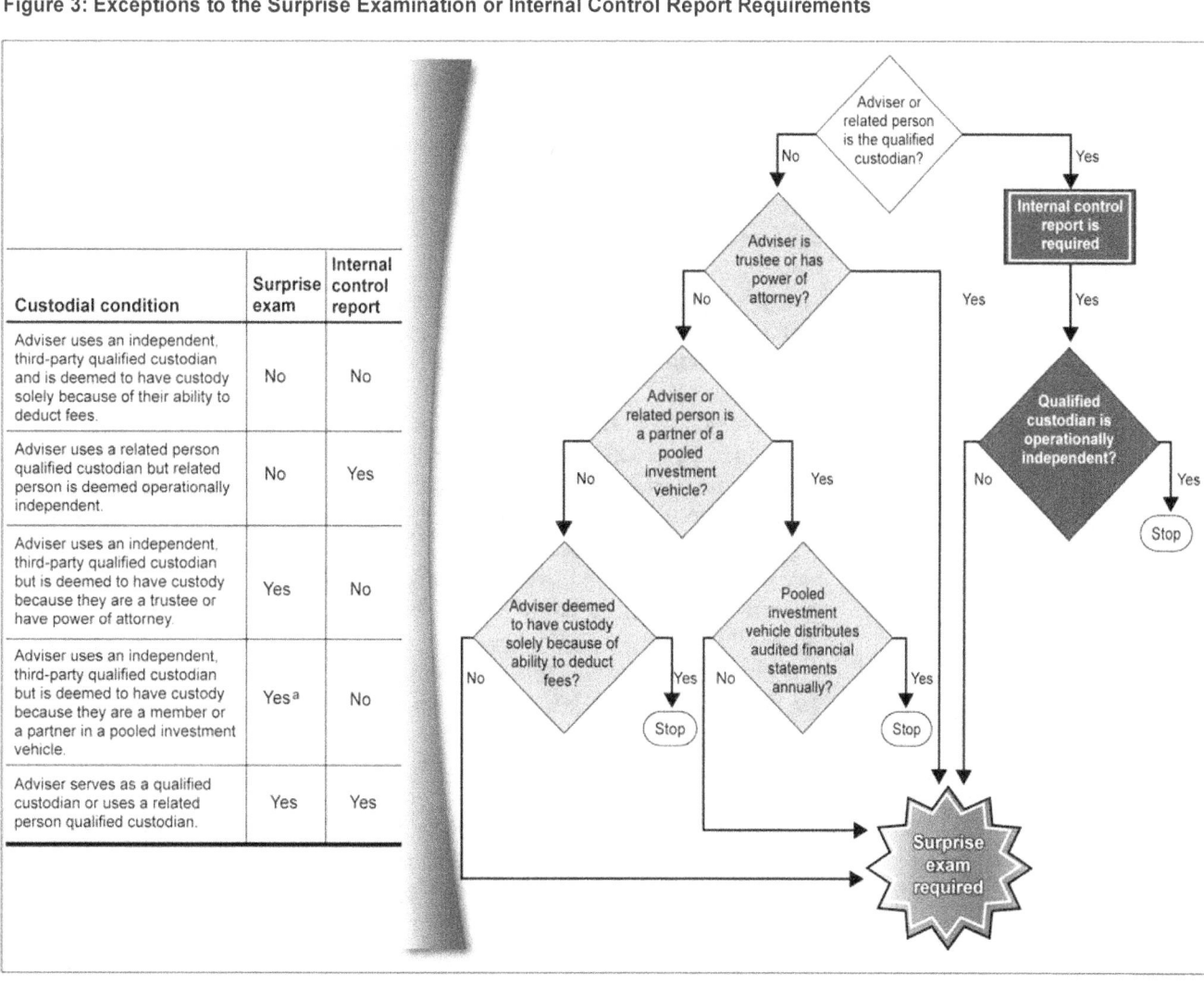

Custodial condition	Surprise exam	Internal control report
Adviser uses an independent, third-party qualified custodian and is deemed to have custody solely because of their ability to deduct fees.	No	No
Adviser uses a related person qualified custodian but related person is deemed operationally independent.	No	Yes
Adviser uses an independent, third-party qualified custodian but is deemed to have custody because they are a trustee or have power of attorney.	Yes	No
Adviser uses an independent, third-party qualified custodian but is deemed to have custody because they are a member or a partner in a pooled investment vehicle.	Yes[a]	No
Adviser serves as a qualified custodian or uses a related person qualified custodian.	Yes	Yes

Source: GAO.

[a]Advisers to pooled investment vehicles may be deemed to comply with the surprise examination requirement of the vehicle if it is audited annually, the audited financial statements are distributed to investors annually, and the auditing is conducted by an independent public accountant that is PCAOB-registered and subject to regular inspection.

Internal Control Reports

Advisers that maintain client assets as the qualified custodian or use a related person qualified custodian rather than maintaining client assets with an independent qualified custodian may present higher risk to clients. In recognition of such risk, SEC also imposed in its 2009 rule amendments a new internal control reporting requirement on advisers that maintain client assets or use related person qualified custodians (see fig. 3 above). The internal control report must include an opinion of an independent public accountant as to whether suitable controls are in place and operating effectively to meet control objectives relating to custodial services. This includes the safeguarding of assets held by the adviser or related person. An adviser that directly maintains client assets as a qualified custodian or maintains client assets with a related person qualified custodian must obtain or receive from its related person an internal control report annually from an accountant that is registered with and subject to regular inspection by PCAOB. Advisers qualifying for a surprise examination exception because of their use of a related person but operationally independent custodian still must obtain an internal control report from their related person.

Related Record-keeping Requirements

In conjunction with the amendments to the custody rule, SEC also amended its record-keeping rule.[27] The revised rule requires advisers to maintain a copy of any internal control report obtained or received pursuant to the SEC custody rule.[28] The rule also requires advisers, if applicable, to maintain a memorandum describing the basis upon which they determined that the presumption that any related person is not operationally independent under the custody rule has been overcome.[29] According to SEC, requiring an adviser to retain a copy of these items provides SEC examiners with important information about the safeguards in place and assists SEC examiners in assessing custody-related risks.

Compliance Requirements and Costs Vary

Around 4,400 advisers, about 45 percent of all SEC-registered advisers, reported having custody (for reasons other than their authority to deduct fees) of over $14 trillion in client assets as of April 1, 2013.[30] In addition, around 500 advisers, about 11 percent of the 4,400 advisers with

---

[27]75 Fed. Reg. 1483 (Jan. 11, 2010) (amending 17 C.F.R. § 275.204-2).

[28]17 C.F.R. § 275.204-2(a)(17)(iii).

[29]17 C.F.R. § 275.204-2(b)(5).

[30]The total reflects advisers that reported they or their related person had custody of client assets. Form ADV does not include a field to track advisers deemed to have custody of client assets solely because of their ability to deduct management fees from client accounts. The total client assets under custody may be overestimated due to advisers that may have erroneously reported duplicate account assets for themselves and a related person.

custody, reported serving as the qualified custodian or having a related person qualified custodian of client assets. As discussed, the SEC custody rule imposes certain minimum requirements generally on all advisers with custody, but not all of the rule's requirements apply to all advisers. Instead, the rule generally imposes more stringent requirements on advisers whose custodial arrangements, in SEC's view, pose greater risk of misappropriation or other misuse of client assets.

According to representatives from industry associations and advisers that we interviewed, advisers can incur an array of direct and indirect costs to comply with the SEC custody rule. Direct costs, such as accounting and legal fees paid by advisers, tend to be more easily measured than indirect costs, such as staff hours spent by an adviser to comply with the rule. The representatives told us that compliance costs include the following:

- Initial costs: After the SEC custody rule was amended in 2009, advisers initially incurred indirect costs (largely management and staff hours) and, in some cases, direct costs (largely consulting or legal fees) to interpret the amendments and comply with the rule's new or amended requirements. For example, one adviser told us that his firm hired a law firm to help it interpret the amended rule, hired a part-time person for 6 months to review and determine over which accounts the adviser had custody, and utilized staff to reprogram the firm's information system to code accounts under custody. Another adviser told us that his firm had the necessary in-house expertise to interpret the amended rule but nevertheless expended considerable internal resources for training staff about the surprise examination requirements and searching for and hiring an accountant to conduct the examinations.
- Recurring costs: On an ongoing basis, advisers incur indirect and, in some cases, direct costs to comply with the custody rule. Advisers expend internal staff hours to maintain records and prepare required statements and disclosures, including Form ADV (the form that advisers use to register with SEC and must update annually). Advisers subject to the surprise examination or internal control report requirement expend staff hours to prepare for and facilitate such reviews. For example, an official from an adviser told us that the firm expends considerable staff hours each year educating the accountant about the firm's operations, generating reports for and providing other support to the accountant, and answering questions from clients related to the examination. In addition, these advisers may incur the direct cost of the examination or audit, and the amount of these fees varies from adviser to adviser (as discussed later in the report).

Although advisers to pooled investment vehicles often undergo an annual financial statement audit in lieu of a surprise examination, they incur the indirect and direct costs associated with the audit.

According to SEC staff and representatives from three industry associations that we spoke with, surprise examinations and internal control reporting, if applicable, tended to be two of the more costly requirements associated with SEC's custody rule. In contrast, record-keeping costs were not significant, according to officials from three associations, two securities law attorneys, and seven of the advisers with whom we spoke.

Cost of Surprise Examinations

According to representatives we interviewed from four accounting firms, their surprise examination fee is based on the amount of hours required to conduct the examinations, which is a function of a number of factors. One of the most important factors is the number of client accounts under custody, which influences the number of accounts that accountants will need to review to verify custody. Other factors affecting examination cost include the amount of client assets under custody, types of securities under custody, and number and location of the custodians. Over 1,300 advisers with custody of client assets, about 30 percent of the 4,400 advisers with custody, reported being subject to the surprise examination requirement as of April 1, 2013. Importantly, these advisers vary widely in terms of the number of their clients under custody—reported by advisers as ranging from 1 client to over 1 million clients—and other factors that affect the cost of surprise examinations. Consequently, the cost of surprise examinations varies widely across the advisers.

Although no comprehensive data exist on surprise examination costs, several industry associations and SEC have provided estimates. In response to SEC's 2009 proposed amendments to the custody rule, industry associations provided SEC with cost estimates. For example, the Investment Advisers Association, representing SEC-registered advisers, estimated that surprise examinations would likely cost each of its members between $20,000 and $300,000. The Securities Industry and Financial Markets Association, representing major asset management firms and custodians, estimated that surprise examination costs would range from $8,000 to $275,000 for each of its members. However, these estimates were based on the then-current SEC guidance to accountants that required verification of 100 percent of client assets under custody. In conjunction with its 2009 final rule amendment, SEC issued a companion release that revised the guidance to allow accountants to verify a sample of client assets.[31] In its 2009 final amendments to the custody rule, SEC estimated the cost of surprise examinations for large, medium, and small advisers in consideration of revisions to its guidance that allowed accountants to verify a sample of client assets. In particular, SEC estimated that the average cost of a surprise examination for large, medium, and small advisers would be $125,000, $20,000, and $10,000, respectively.[32]

To help determine the range of potential costs of surprise examinations for selected subgroups of advisers, we obtained data on the examination fees for 12 advisers.[33] As shown in figure 4, the fees that the 12 advisers paid to their independent public accountants for recent surprise examinations ranged from $3,500 to $31,000. Figure 4 also shows that fees varied among advisers we selected within each of the subgroups. For example, fees in subgroup 2 ranged from $3,500 to $16,000 for the three advisers we selected.[34]

---

[31]Commission Guidance Regarding Independent Public Accountant Engagements Performed Pursuant to Rule 206(4)-2, Investment Advisers Act Release No. 2969, 97 SEC Docket 1896 (Dec. 30, 2009). According to SEC, the commenters based their cost estimates for surprise examinations on the previous guidance for accountants, which required verification of 100 percent of client assets. SEC expects that the estimates would be significantly lower if they reflected the current procedures for the surprise examination, which allows for the use of sampling of client accounts. The current procedures were described in the guidance for accountants issued in a companion release and became effective March 12, 2010.

[32]75 Fed. Reg. at 1473. SEC defined large firms as those advisers subject to a surprise examination that either served as a qualified custodian or had a related person serve as a qualified custodian. The remaining firms subject to the surprise examinations were defined as small or medium based on the number of their clients relative to the average number of clients for the entire group.

[33]For additional information, see appendix I.

[34]Our cost data may not be indicative of the examination costs of other advisers in the same subgroup because factors other than the number of clients and assets under custody can affect costs. In addition, because we selected advisers near each subgroup's median value, we did not obtain cost data from the largest advisers, whose examination costs may be closer in line with SEC's $125,000 cost estimate for large advisers.

Figure 4: Surprise Examination Costs for 12 SEC-Registered Investment Advisers, 2012

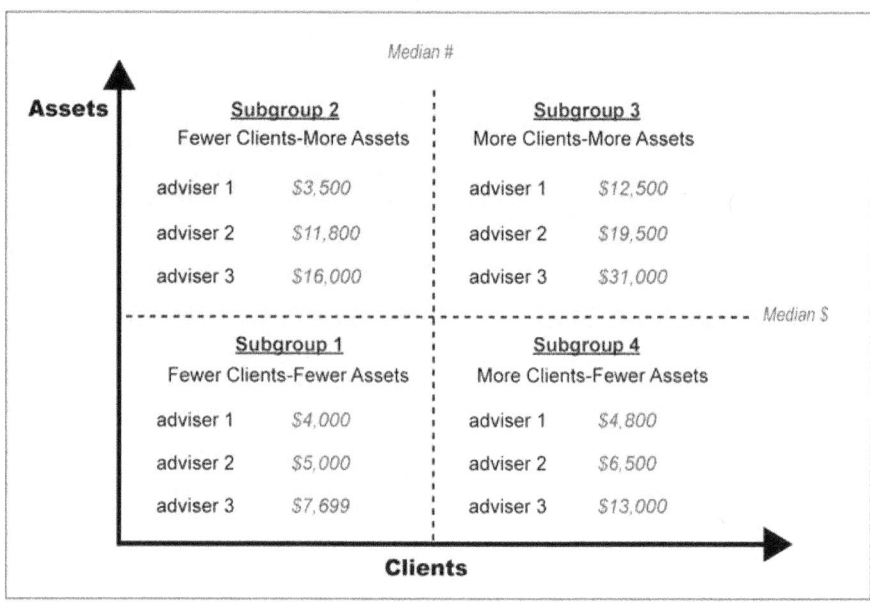

Source: GAO analysis of SEC-registered adviser and accountant interviews.

Note: Based on Form ADV data as of December 2012, approximately 1,300 advisers reported undergoing surprise examinations. We divided these advisers into four subgroups based on whether the number of their clients under custody and amount of their client assets under custody were above or below the group's median value for the two variables. Thus, at one end of the spectrum, subgroup 1 includes advisers whose number of clients and amount of client assets under custody were both below the group's median values. At the other end of the spectrum, subgroup 3 includes advisers whose number of clients and amount of client assets were both above the group's median values. Within each subgroup, we then selected advisers whose client assets were around the subgroup's median value. (For additional information see app. I.)

Cost of Internal Control Reports

Fewer than 500 advisers, about 11 percent of advisers with custody, reported obtaining internal control reports as of April 1, 2013. Similar to surprise examination costs, the cost of internal control reports varies based on a number of factors, such as the size of and services offered by the qualified custodian. In its final 2009 rule, SEC estimated that an internal control report relating to custody would cost, on average, $250,000.[35] According to officials from four accounting firms we spoke with, internal control reporting costs for their clients may range from $25,000 to $500,000. Unlike with surprise examinations and associated

---

[35]75 Fed. Reg. at 1482.

costs, some advisers and their related person qualified custodians may obtain internal control reports for reasons other than the custody rule. For example, representatives from two industry associations told us that institutional investors commonly require their custodians that are related persons to their advisers to obtain internal control reports.[36]

SEC Views Advisers Using Related but Operationally Independent Custodians as Posing Relatively Low Risk

SEC provided certain investment advisers with an exception from the surprise examination requirement because their custodial practices pose relatively lower risk or they adopted other controls to protect client assets, such as annual financial statement audits. The broad range of industry, regulatory, and other parties that we interviewed generally supported or did not have a view on the surprise examination exception provided to advisers using related but operationally independent custodians to hold client assets.

SEC Excepted Advisers from Surprise Examination Requirement for Several Reasons

Although SEC's 2009 proposed amendments to the custody rule would have required all registered advisers with custody of client assets to undergo a surprise examination, SEC provided exceptions from the requirement to certain advisers in the final 2009 rule amendments. In the 2009 amendments, SEC expressed that the surprise examination requirement should help deter fraud because advisers will know their client assets are subject to verification at any time and, thus, may be less likely to engage in misconduct.[37] SEC noted that if fraud does occur, the examination will increase the likelihood that the fraud will be detected earlier.[38]

As discussed earlier, advisers deemed to have custody solely because of their authority to deduct fees from client accounts are excluded from the surprise examination requirement. In SEC's view, the magnitude of the risks of client losses from overcharging advisory fees did not warrant the costs of obtaining a surprise examination. Also excluded from the

---

[36]Similarly, in its 2009 proposed amendments to the custody rule, SEC stated that it understood that mutual fund custodians obtain internal control reports for other reasons. 74 Fed. Reg. at 25,370 n.165.

[37]75 Fed. Reg. at 1475.

[38]*Id.*

requirement are advisers to a pooled investment vehicle that undergo annual audits of their financial statements by an independent public accountant and distribute the audited statements to investors. According to SEC, procedures performed by accountants during the course of a financial statement audit provide meaningful protections to investors, and the surprise examination would not significantly add to these protections.[39]

Additionally, SEC provided a limited exception to advisers that are (1) deemed to have custody solely because a related person serves as the custodian and holds client assets and (2) operationally independent of the custodian. According to SEC, client assets may be at greater risk when maintained by an adviser's related person. However, SEC noted that firms under common ownership but operationally independent of each other present substantially lower client custodial risks than those that are not.[40] According to SEC, the risk is lower because the misuse of client assets would tend to require collusion between the adviser and custodian employees, which is not significantly different than would be necessary to engage in similar misconduct between unaffiliated organizations.[41] Under the custody rule, a related person is presumed not to be operationally independent unless each of the following conditions is met and no other circumstances can reasonably be expected to compromise the operational independence of the related person:

- client assets in the custody of the related person are not subject to claims of the adviser's creditors;
- advisory personnel do not have custody or possession of, or direct or indirect access to, client assets of which the related person has custody, or the power to control the disposition of such client assets to third parties for the benefit of the adviser or its related persons, or otherwise have the opportunity to misappropriate such client assets;

---

[39]The financial statement audit must be prepared in accordance with generally accepted accounting principles and the audit must be done in accordance with generally accepted auditing standards. In a financial statement audit, the accountant performs procedures comparable to those that would be performed in a surprise examination, including verifying the existence of funds and securities and obtaining confirmation from investors.

[40]75 Fed. Reg. at 1464.

[41]*Id.*

- advisory personnel and personnel of the related person who have access to advisory client assets are not under common supervision; and
- advisory personnel do not hold any position with the related person or share premises with the related person.[42]

Although an adviser that meets these conditions would not be required to undergo a surprise examination, the adviser still would be required to comply with the rule's other applicable provisions, including obtaining an internal control report from its related person. SEC emphasized that an adviser that has custody due to reasons in addition to a related person having custody cannot rely on the exception because it is only applicable if an adviser has custody solely because its related person has custody. For example, an adviser that has custody because he or she serves as a trustee with respect to client assets held in an account at a broker-dealer that is a related person could not rely on the exception from the surprise examination on the grounds that the broker-dealer was operationally independent, because the adviser has custody for reasons other than through its operationally independent related person.

A Limited Number of Advisers Do Not Undergo Surprise Examinations Because They Use Related but Operationally Independent Custodians

As of April 1, 2013, 169 registered advisers reported having custody of client assets and using related but operationally independent custodians and not undergoing an annual surprise examination for certain clients.[43] These advisers account for around 2 percent of all SEC-registered advisers and about 42 percent of the approximately 400 SEC-registered advisers that have a related person holding client assets. These advisers collectively have over $6 trillion in regulatory assets under management and custody of over $1 trillion of client assets. The structure of large institutions with functionally independent subsidiaries tends to lend itself to meet the operationally independent conditions. More specifically, we identified some advisers using related but operationally independent custodians that are part of large financial institutions with numerous subsidiaries, such as Deutsche Bank, JPMorgan Chase, Morgan Stanley,

---

[42]17 C.F.R. § 275.206(4)-2(d)(5).

[43]Of the 169 registered investment advisers, 41 of them qualified for an exception from the surprise examination requirement for some of their clients under custody but underwent a surprise examination for other clients under custody. For example, an adviser might have custody of certain client assets because it solely held such assets with a related but operationally independent client but may have custody of other client assets because it served as a trustee for those accounts.

GAO-13-569 SEC Custody Rule Costs

and Wells Fargo. According to SEC staff, this outcome is to be expected given that the adviser and custodian staff cannot be considered operationally independent while under common supervision and sharing the same premises.

If advisers currently qualifying for an exception from the surprise examination requirement were required to undergo such examinations, the costs of the examinations would likely vary considerably across the advisers. Like advisers currently subject to the surprise examination requirement, advisers excepted from the requirement vary considerably in terms of the factors that affect the cost of the examinations. For example, the number of clients these advisers had under custody ranged from 1 client to over 500,000 clients, as of April 1, 2013. Similarly, the amount of client assets under their custody ranged from $680,000 to $320 billion.

Views on the Surprise Examination's Exception and Effectiveness

The broad range of industry, accounting firms, and other parties we interviewed largely told us that they either support or do not have a view on the surprise examination exception. However, several of these representatives said that the exception's operationally independent conditions were too stringent or difficult to meet.[44] None of the investment advisers we interviewed use a related custodian to hold client assets, and most did not have a view on the exception or SEC's rationale. The North American Securities Administrators Association (NASAA) staff told us that when a custodian is a related person of the adviser, ensuring that the adviser meets and complies with the operationally independent conditions would require the firm to conduct a thorough analysis of its operations and any changes that may affect the custodian's operational independence. The staff further noted that NASAA's custody model rule for use by state securities regulators, unlike the SEC custody rule, does not include an exception from the surprise examination requirement based on the concept of operational independence between an

---

[44]The officials said the requirements that both adviser and custodian staff cannot (1) be under common supervision and (2) share the same premises were examples of conditions that were difficult to meet. More specifically, one official told us that a number of large banks have related advisers and custodians that share a building but are located on different floors and thus would have to move staff to another building to qualify for the exception.

investment adviser and a custodian that is a related person.[45] An investor advocacy representative told us that he generally opposes allowing advisers to use related custodians, but if that were allowed, he said that, in his opinion, the surprise examination exception would be appropriate for only large, complex entities subject to existing regulation, such as banks and broker-dealers.

Many of the industry, regulatory, and other parties we interviewed agreed with SEC's view that surprise examinations can help to deter fraud. However, some told us that one of the examination's weaknesses is that accountants must rely on advisers to provide them with a complete list of the client assets under custody to verify. According to some of these representatives, an adviser defrauding a client could omit that client's account from the list provided to the accountant to avoid detection. Officials from an accounting firm told us that no infallible procedure exists to test the completeness of the client list, given that the list must come from the adviser. According to SEC staff, an adviser with custody and intent on defrauding its clients also may not register with SEC or, if it does, may not report that it has custody of client assets or hire an accountant to conduct a surprise examination. SEC staff also noted that the surprise examination requirement, like any regulation, cannot prevent fraud 100 percent of the time but that it helps deter such misconduct.

SEC data indicate that surprise examinations have identified compliance issues and helped target higher-risk advisers for examination. SEC staff told us that since the 2009 custody rule amendments became effective in March 2010, auditors conducting surprise examinations have found around 100 advisers with one or more instances of material noncompliance with the rule, such as failing to maintain client securities at a qualified custodian. According to SEC staff, the results of surprise examinations serve as an early warning of potential risks and are used by staff to help assess the risk level of advisers and, in turn, select advisers for SEC examination. For example, in March 2013, SEC's Office of Compliance Inspections and Examinations issued a "Risk Alert" that noted that about 33 percent (over 140 examinations) of recent SEC

---

[45]NASAA Model Custody Rule under the Uniform Securities Act of 1956 (amended Apr. 15, 2013). NASAA Model Custody Rule under the Uniform Securities Act of 2002 (amended Apr. 15, 2013).

examinations found custody-related deficiencies.[46] These deficiencies included failures to comply with the rule's surprise examination requirement and qualified custodian requirements and resulted in actions ranging from immediate remediation to enforcement referrals and subsequent litigation.

Agency Comments

We requested comments from SEC, but none were provided. SEC provided technical comments, which we incorporated, as appropriate.

We are sending copies of this report to SEC, interested congressional committees and members, and others. The report also is available at no charge on the GAO website at http://www.gao.gov.

If you or your staffs have any questions about this report, please contact me at (202) 512-8678 or clowersa@gao.gov. Contact points for our Offices of Congressional Relations and Public Affairs may be found on the last page of this report. GAO staff who made major contributions to this report are listed in appendix II.

A. Nicole Clowers
Director
Financial Markets and Community Investment Issues

---

[46]SEC's Office of Compliance Inspections and Examinations, National Exam Program Risk Alert, *Significant Deficiencies Involving Adviser Custody and Safety of Client Assets*, vol. 3, issue 1 (Mar. 4, 2013).

Appendix I: Objectives, Scope, and Methodology

This report describes (1) the requirements of and costs associated with the Securities and Exchange Commission (SEC) custody rule, including any related record-keeping requirements, for registered investment advisers, and (2) SEC's rationale for not requiring advisers using related but operationally independent custodians to undergo surprise examinations, and the number and characteristics of such advisers.

To address both objectives, we analyzed SEC's record-keeping and custody rules under the Investment Advisers Act of 1940 to document compliance requirements (e.g., surprise examinations and internal control reports) for SEC-registered investment advisers. Furthermore, we reviewed proposed and final SEC amendments to the custody rule, comment letters, and other information, such as GAO and other studies, to analyze how and why the custody rule requirements have changed, particularly the surprise examination requirement and exceptions, and obtain information on compliance costs. We analyzed publicly available data in the Investment Adviser Registration Depository (IARD) to identify the number of SEC-registered investment advisers and information advisers reported about their compliance with the SEC custody rule's requirements. IARD data are submitted by advisers in Form ADV, which is used by advisers to register with SEC and must be updated annually by advisers.[1] We assessed the reliability of Form ADV data by interviewing SEC staff and testing the data for errors, and we determined the data were sufficiently reliable for our purposes. Specifically, we interviewed SEC staff about the IARD database and Form ADV to understand how the data are collected, what types of edit checks are incorporated into the system, and the staff's overall views of the system's data reliability with respect to our purposes. We also performed electronic testing to identify potential errors, and we discussed analysis methodology considerations, such as excluding particular records, with SEC staff for any inconsistencies that we identified. For the purposes of our final analysis, we excluded records for advisers that reported zero as the regulatory assets under management or total clients and any record with the latest Form ADV filing date older than January 2012.

---

[1]Form ADV consists of two parts. Part 1 collects information about the adviser's business, ownership, clients, employees, business practices (especially those involving potential conflicts with clients), and any disciplinary events of the adviser or its employees. Part 2 collects information required in client brochures and brochure supplements.

To obtain data on the costs of complying with the SEC custody rule, particularly its surprise examination and internal control report requirements, and other information, we interviewed a limited number of investment advisers and accounting firms. Based on Form ADV data as of December 3, 2012, we identified approximately 1,300 advisers that reported undergoing surprise examinations. To systematically target advisers and firms, we first divided the total group of advisers that reported undergoing surprise examinations into four subgroups based on whether the amount of their client assets under custody were above or below the group's median value of approximately $101 million and whether their number of clients under custody were above or below the median of 19 clients, as shown in figure 5. Thus, at one end of the spectrum, subgroup 1 includes advisers whose number of clients and amount of client assets under custody were both below the group's median values. At the other end of the spectrum, subgroup 3 includes advisers whose number of clients and amount of client assets were both above the group's median values. Within each subgroup, we then selected advisers whose client assets were around the subgroup's median value. For the 12 selected advisers, we interviewed eight of the advisers and interviewed four accountants who conducted the surprise examinations for the other four advisers.

Figure 5: SEC-Registered Advisers That Underwent Surprise Examinations by Number of Client Accounts and Client Assets under Custody, as of December 3, 2012

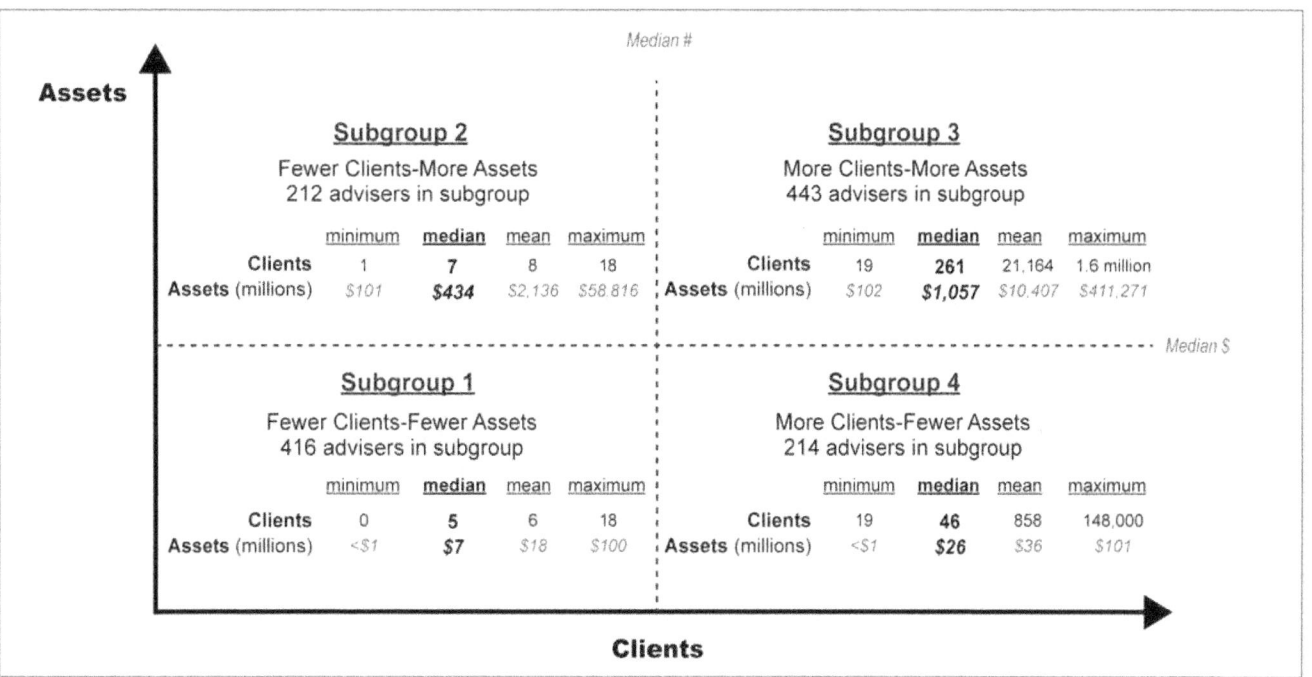

Source: GAO analysis of Form ADV data as of December 3, 2012

To obtain information on the cost of complying with the custody rule and other information, we also interviewed regulators, including SEC staff, officials from the North American Securities Administrators Association, and a representative from a state securities authority, and representatives from investment adviser, accountant, investor advocacy, and other associations, including the American Institute of Certified Public Accountants, American Bankers Association, Financial Services Institute, Fund Democracy, Investment Advisers Association, Managed Futures Association, Private Equity Growth and Capital Council, and Securities Industry and Financial Markets Association. In addition, we interviewed two securities law attorneys.

We conducted this performance audit from September 2012 through July 2013 in accordance with generally accepted government auditing standards. Those standards require that we plan and perform the audit to obtain sufficient, appropriate evidence to provide a reasonable basis for our findings and conclusions based on our audit objectives. We believe that the evidence obtained provides a reasonable basis for our findings and conclusions based on our audit objectives.

Appendix II: GAO Contact and Staff Acknowledgments

GAO Contact	A. Nicole Clowers, (202) 512-8678 or clowersa@gao.gov
Staff Acknowledgments	In addition to the individual named above, Richard Tsuhara, Assistant Director; Carl Barden; William Chatlos; F. Chase Cook; Kristen Kociolek; Risto Laboski; Grant Mallie; Patricia Moye; Jennifer Schwartz; Jena Sinkfield; and Verginie Tarpinian made major contributions to this report.

www.ingramcontent.com/pod-product-compliance
Lightning Source LLC
Chambersburg PA
CBHW080745290526
45790CB00008B/3334

* 9 7 8 1 5 0 3 1 9 9 6 6 8 *